Your Declaration of Dependence on God

Thou shalt also decree a thing, and it shall be established unto thee: and the light shall shine upon thy ways.

Job 22:28

Dr. Jacquelyn Hadnot

Your Declaration of Dependence on God

Your Declaration of Dependence on God
Dr. Jacquelyn Hadnot
Published by: Igniting the Fire Publishing
1314 North 38th Street
Kansas City, KS 66102
www.ignitingthefire.net

No part of this publication may be reproduced, stored in a retrieval system, or transmitted, in any form or by any means, electronic, mechanical, photocopying, recording, or otherwise, without the written prior permission of the author.

Unless otherwise noted, all Scripture quotations are taken from King James Version of the Bible.

Scripture quotations marked AMP are taken from The Amplified Bible AMP. The Amplified Bible, Old Testament copyright © 1965, 1987 by the Zondervan Corporation. The Amplified New Testament, copyright © 1954, 1958, 1987 by the Lockman Foundation. Used by permission.

Scripture quotations marked NASB are taken from The New American Standard Bible AMP. Copyright © 1960, 1962, 1963, 1968, 1971, 1972, 1973, 1975, 1977 by the Zondervan Corporation. The Amplified New Testament, copyright © 1954, 1958, 1987 by the Lockman Foundation. Used by permission.

Scripture quotations marked NIV are taken from The New International Version. Copyright © 1973, 1978, 1984 by the International Bible Society. Used by permission.

Cover Design: Dr. Jacquelyn Hadnot
Copyright© 2012 by Dr. Jacquelyn Hadnot
All rights reserved.

Please note that Igniting the Fire's publishing style capitalizes certain pronouns in Scripture that refer to the Father, Son, and Holy Spirit, and may differ from some Bible publishers' styles.

ISBN 9780615477909

All rights reserved under International Copyright Law.
Contents and/or cover may not be reproduced in whole or in part in any form without the expressed written consent of the Publisher.

Your Declaration of Dependence on God

Table of Contents

Dedication 4
Contents of the Workbook 5
Introduction...How to Use This Workbook 6

Chapter 1
　　Your Declaration of Dependence on God 7

Chapter 2
　　The Power of the Tongue 9

Chapter 3
　　Word Worth 13

Chapter 4
　　Your Journey Begins 15

Chapter 5
　　Questions to Begin Your Journey 19
　　Questions Journal Space 21

Chapter 6
　　Begin Each Day with a Declaration 27

Chapter 7
　　52 Declarations of Dependence of God 29

Chapter 8
　　Stand and See the Salvation of the Lord 59

Chapter 9
　　Prayer for Breaking Word Curses 63

Chapter 10
　　Declaration Journals 65

Chapter 11
　　Scriptures on Prayer 117

Declarative Prayers 121
Appendix: Self Life 130
About the Author 131
Others Books 133
Declaration Agreement to Share with Others 137

Dedication

This book is dedicated to My Lord and Savior Jesus Christ.
Thank you for revealing the power of the tongue.

Death and life are in the power of the tongue: and they that love it shall eat the fruit thereof. (Proverbs 18:21)

To everyone with a desire to walk in victory.

To every minister of the Gospel who has given their life to spreading the uncompromising message of Jesus Christ and His precious gift to us.

Your Declaration of Dependence on God

What is in this workbook

Within the pages of this workbook, you will find:

- 52 Declarations to pray over your life, children, spouse, family members, co-workers, etc.
- Declaration journals.
- Questions to ask yourself as you begin your journey.
- Prayer of Salvation.
- Scriptures that provide a foundation for your declarations.
- Understanding the power of the tongue.
- Prayer for breaking word curses from your past.
- Examples of self-life issues that hinder your destiny.

Every area of our lives should begin and end with the Word of God. In other words, what does God have to say about the matter?

Many blessings on your road to discovery. I pray that every moment you spend in His presence is renewing, reviving and refreshing. Enjoy the journey.

Your Declaration of Dependence on God

How to use this workbook

The most effective way to use this workbook and each declaration is:

1. Read the declaration of the week 3 times each day.
2. Read the scriptures at the bottom of the declaration 3 times.
3. Pray the declaration and insert your name, spouse, and children where necessary.
4. Stay with each declaration for at least a week. Speaking it daily, praying for ways to change the behavior or situation.
5. Post the declaration in places you can read it during the day.
6. Journal the desired outcome as you approach the end of the week.
7. If you need more time, stay with the declaration until the desired outcome has been reached.
8. Speak life into every situation you encounter.
9. Keep a journal of the negative words you have spoken over the years and ask the Lord to show you the changes He desires.
10. Ask the Lord to reveal all the negative, dry places in your life. Ask Him to give you a declaration to pray.

Chapter 1  Your Declaration of Dependence on God

Job 22:28 tells us, Thou shalt also decree a thing, and it shall be established unto thee: and the light shall shine upon thy ways. As children of the Most High God, we must begin to declare or speak into the atmosphere what our God has spoken to us concerning our destiny. *For I know the thoughts that I think toward you, saith the LORD, thoughts of peace, and not of evil, to give you an expected end* (Jeremiah 29:11). We must not allow the enemy to plant words of defeat and death. We must approach the each day with a holy determination to speak those things…

Declaring all that the Lord has for us in this new season means taking a new approach to the doors God has for us. We must cancel every demonic assignment against us and close doors that have become a hindrance to us. *For we wrestle not against flesh and blood, but against principalities, against powers, against the rulers of the darkness of this world, against spiritual wickedness in high places* (Ephesians 6:12).

Your Declaration of Dependence on God

We must decree and declare the thoughts and plans of the Lord for our lives. Never again walking in fear or doubt, but trusting God through all, in all and for all. The worst thing we can do is to speak death to our future by believing the report of the enemy. Whose report will you believe?

Jesus said, "I am come that they might have life, and that they might have it more abundantly" in John 10:10. Abundant life has no limits or boundaries. Just as our relationship with the Lord is limitless and endless, our future should have no limits. Each day we should strive to reach our full potential.

As we begin to take a spiritual inventory of our lives, we must examine the canvas we have painted over the years. In doing so, we must look honestly at the picture we have painted and ask, "Is this the view that God desires for me? Am I in a place where God can bless me? Am I missing His fullness?"

If you answered no, it is okay because this book is for you. It is a guide to help you address the way we walk out our destiny by addressing one of the biggest hindrances to our destiny - the **tongue**. The tongue has more power than many of us realize. It carries life and death. The tongue can kill your destiny quicker than cancer. What tool can the enemy use against you? **<u>Your tongue.</u>**

Chapter 2  The Power of the Tongue

When we come to realize that life and death is in the power of the tongue, we will be careful with the words that flow from our mouth. *"Death and life are in the power of the tongue: and they that love it shall eat the fruit thereof"* (Proverbs 18:21). Choose to speak life or speak death. An unbridled tongue will unleash death and destruction into your life and the lives of your loved ones. Have you ever considered the fact that your negative declarations anger the Lord and shut up the windows of heaven in your life? *"Because you rage against me and your insolence has reached my ears, I will put my hook in your nose and my bit in your mouth, and I will make you return by the way you came"* (2 Kings 19:28).

The Bible tells us in Ephesians 4:27 to give no place to the devil. It is unfortunate that we give the devil a free ride when we begin to speak negatively about our situations. We say things such as:

- ➢ I will always be broke.
- ➢ I will never get out of debt.

Your Declaration of Dependence on God

- My husband will never be saved.
- My kids will never amount to anything.
- I am so dumb, I will never be able to learn.
- I am never going to be happy.
- I will always be sick.
- I will always be on welfare or government assistance.
- I will always be tormented by my past.
- I will never get off drugs or alcohol.
- I have been lazy all my life I will never change.
- My situation is hopeless, I cannot do anything about it.

Sound familiar? At some time in life, we have made a negative statement or declaration. In other words spoken death over our circumstances. What a shame!

We give the enemy ammunition to wage war against us when we speak death, destruction and disease into the atmosphere. Do you think any of our destructive statements are acceptable to God? I think not. Jesus said that He came to give us an abundant life. The tricks, lies and deceptions of the enemy have nothing to do with abundance. The enemy's deceptions are designed to negate the abundant life that Jesus desires for us. If this attitude is left unchecked, we can fall into the trap of unbelief. *If ye will not believe, surely ye shall not be established* (Isaiah 7:9).

Your Declaration of Dependence on God

Unbelief is a hindrance to the power of God in your life. Not only does it stop the flow of God's power, it also stops the flow of God's blessings. It binds the individual to a life of mediocrity. Unbelief is equal to rebellion and no one can enter into the presence of the Lord with unbelief on his heart. Belief requires faith and without faith, it is impossible to please God. *"And without faith it is impossible to please God, because anyone who comes to him must believe that he exists and that he rewards those who earnestly seek Him"* (Hebrews 11:6).

I believe that if we have a declaration for each week of the year, the process for renewing our mind would become a year round journey. *Your Declaration of Dependence on God* is a road map to begin decreeing and declaring the fullness of God into your life. A tool to stop the downward spiral of negative thinking and speaking.

I pray that as you read and meditate on each declaration you will find wisdom, knowledge and the motivation to renew your mind. Moreover, be not conformed to this world: but be ye transformed by the renewing of your mind, that ye may prove what is that good, and acceptable, and perfect, will of God (Romans 12:2).

Your Declaration of Dependence on God

Chapter 3

Word Worth

The following definitions will assist you in understanding each word as it pertains to our subject matter.

Decree means *official order: an order with the power of legislation issued by a ruler or other person or group with authority, anything settled or unchangeable.*

    Example: The decree was issued to dissolve the partnership.

Declare means *announce something clearly or loudly: to state something in a plain, open, or emphatic way.*

    Example: We must begin to declare financial prosperity as we walk through the recession.

Declaration means *making of declaration: the process or act of declaring something in an official or public way.*

    Example: My declaration for the new year is to stand on God's Word.

Your Declaration of Dependence on God

Establish means: *cause plant to grow successfully: to grow, or cause a plant to grow, successfully in a new place.*

Example: I will establish myself in a Bible believing church.

Begin each day with prayer. Man should always pray. *"Do not be anxious about anything, but in everything, by prayer and petition, with thanksgiving, present your requests to God"* (Philippians 4:6). *"Devote yourselves to prayer, being watchful and thankful"* (Colossians 4:2). *"The prayer of a righteous man is powerful and effective"* (James 5:16).

Chapter 4  Your Journey Begins

As the journey begins, keep in mind that this is not a quick fix to your problems, a magic formula to speak over your life or a "tah dah" remedy to dissolve years of "stinking thinking" and a "venomous tongue." It is however, a tool that God can use to help you begin speaking, praying and thinking your new life in Christ through the power of your tongue.

> **Word Wealth**
>
> **Trust** is defined as confidence in and reliance on good qualities, especially fairness, truth, honor or ability.

I pray that this book will become the road map to move you to another level of thinking, praying, faith and trust in God. The Bibles tells us in Proverbs 3:5-6 that you must *"Trust in the LORD with all your heart and lean not on your own understanding; in all your ways acknowledge him, and he will make your paths straight."* If we avoid our carnal or flesh driven wisdom, the Lord will bring health to our lives. *"Do not be wise in your own eyes; fear the LORD and shun evil. This will bring health to your body and nourishment to your bones"* (Proverbs 3:7-8).

Your Declaration of Dependence on God

The Lord has designed this workbook to be interactive. As you read each declaration, a response is required. The response is a personal prayer to be written in the back of the book. There is also space in the back for journaling your thoughts and prayers.

You must be honest with yourself if this workbook is to be an effective tool for renewing your mind and transforming your life into a life that God can use. Each day you walk out your front door you are a "living sacrifice" that means walking in holiness, righteousness and being acceptable to God. *I beseech you therefore, brethren, by the mercies of God, that ye present your bodies a living sacrifice, holy, acceptable unto God, which is your reasonable service. And be not conformed to this world: but be ye transformed by the renewing of your mind, that ye may prove what is that good, and acceptable, and perfect, will of God. For I say, through the grace given unto me, to every man that is among you, not to think of himself more highly than he ought to think; but to think soberly, according as God hath dealt to every man the measure of faith* (Romans 12:1-3).

We can never lie to God, we only lie to ourselves. Self-deceit is a very dangerous weapon the enemy will use against us. It renders us ineffective in most situations because we are unwilling to face the truth. Remember, when it comes to the ultimate deception you are dealing with the master deceiver, Satan. *"For we wrestle not against flesh and blood, but against principalities, against powers, against the rulers of the darkness of this world, against spiritual wickedness in high places"* (Ephesians 6:12). Make no mistake about it, Satan is out to deceive you: kill your joy, steal

Your Declaration of Dependence on God

your destiny and destroy your testimony for Christ Jesus. Therefore, you must not be deceived into thinking, speaking, or acting on his lies and deceptions.

The bible warns us to "Be Not Deceived."

- Take heed to yourselves, that your heart be not deceived, and ye turn aside, and serve other gods, and worship them (Deut. 11:16).

- Let not him that is deceived trust in vanity: for vanity shall be his recompense (Job 15:31).

- Know ye not that the unrighteous shall not inherit the kingdom of God? Be not deceived: neither fornicators, nor idolaters, nor adulterers, nor effeminate, nor abusers of themselves with mankind (1Corinthians 6:9).

- Be not deceived: evil communications corrupt good manners (1Corintians 15:33).

- Be not deceived; God is not mocked: for whatsoever a man soweth, that shall he also reap (Galatians 6:7).

- …whosoever is deceived thereby is not wise (Proverbs 20:1).

Arm yourself with the full armor of God and stand against the wiles, tricks and manipulations of the devil. Having done all, stand and watch the Lord bring a great victory in your life. *"Wherefore take unto you the whole armour of God, that ye may be able to withstand in the evil day, and having done all, to stand. Stand therefore, having your loins girt about with truth,*

Your Declaration of Dependence on God

and having on the breastplate of righteousness; And your feet shod with the preparation of the gospel of peace; Above all, taking the shield of faith, wherewith ye shall be able to quench all the fiery darts of the wicked. And take the helmet of salvation, and the sword of the Spirit, which is the word of God: Praying always with all prayer and supplication in the Spirit, and watching thereunto with all perseverance and supplication for all saints" (Ephesians 6:13-18).

Begin each day with Prayer

The prayers of a righteous man is powerful and effective.

(James 5:16)

Chapter 5 ❓ Questions to Begin Your Journey

- Do you believe that you are receiving the fullness of God?
- Do you find yourself easily distracted by the trappings of the world? Example: drugs, gambling, unmarried sex, cursing, lying, excessive shopping, pornography, too much television, explicit music and movies.
- Have you ever been told that you are a negative person?
- Do you see all your decisions as bad ones?
- Are you spiritually lazy?
- Do you find it hard to finish an assignment?
- Do you long for a better life?
- Are you struggling with the desire to leave church?
- Do you blame others for your problems?
- Do you struggle with un-forgiveness?
- Do you feel as if your life is hopeless?
- Do you struggle with low self-esteem?
- Have you asked God to reveal your self-life issues? (See the Appendix)
- Does anger easily rise within you when faced with a problem?
- Do you struggle with asking others for help?

Your Declaration of Dependence on God

- Are you ashamed of your current situation: financial, physical, emotional, mental, etc.?
- Do you feel as if God does not hear your prayers?
- Are memories of abusive relationships hindering your future?
- How much time do you spend in prayer?
- Do you look forward to going to church?
- How much time do you spend reading the Word of God?
- Do you find it difficult to pray?
- Do you find it difficult to say nice things about yourself?
- Do you find it difficult to say nice things about others?
- Are you angry with God?

Approach each question with a desire to grow deeper in your life, deeper in the Word of God and a deeper relationship with Him.

Prayer

*Now, O Lord God, confirm forever the word You have given to me (**Your Name Here**) Your servant and my house; and do as You have said, And Your name [and presence] shall be magnified forever, saying, The Lord of hosts is God over my life; and the house of Your servant (**Your Name Here**) will be made firm before You. For You, O Lord of hosts, have revealed this to me. So Your servant has found courage to pray this prayer to You. And now, O Lord God, You are God, Your words are truth, and You have promised this good thing to me. Therefore, now let it please You to bless the house of Your servant, that it may continue forever before You; for You, O Lord God, have spoken it, and with Your blessing let [my] house be blessed forever. In Jesus Name. Amen.*

Your Declaration of Dependence on God

Journal Space for Your Answers

Your Declaration of Dependence on God

Your Declaration of Dependence on God

Your Declaration of Dependence on God

Your Declaration of Dependence on God

Your Declaration of Dependence on God

Chapter 6 — Begin Each Day with a Declaration

Other than prayer, nothing starts your day off to a good start like a declaration of victory. Declaring the blessings of God, the favor of God and the hand of God over your life, children, spouse or family will open the door to walking in victory over any situation. **SOUND THE TRUMPET OF VICTORY!!**

1. Read the declaration of the week 3 times each day.
2. Read the scriptures at the bottom of the declaration 3 times.
3. Pray the declaration and insert your name, spouse and children where necessary.
4. Stay with each declaration for at least a week. Speaking it daily, praying for ways to change the behavior or situation.
5. Post the declaration in places you can read it during the day.
6. Journal the desired outcome as you approach the end of the week.
7. If you need more time, stay with the declaration until the desired outcome has been reached.
8. Speak life into every situation you encounter.
9. Keep a journal of the negative words you have spoken over the years and ask the Lord to show you the changes He desires.

Your Declaration of Dependence on God

10. Ask the Lord to reveal all the negative, dry places in your life.

11. Ask Him to give you a declaration to pray for every obstacle.

12. As you enter this covenant with God begin to speak over every situation, please keep in mind that you have what you say you have. If you want victory, declare V I C T O R Y in the Name of Jesus.

13. Do not become discouraged when change does not come instantly, negative habits did not happen over night.

14. Believe God for every Word He has spoken into your life.

15. Enjoy the journey of discovering a new you through Christ Jesus.

16. Finally, speak those things that be not as though they are.

Chapter 7

52

Declarations of Dependence on God

I agree that from this day forward I will begin to speak life into every situation I encounter. I will decree a thing and it will be established for me by Christ Jesus. I declare that I represent the King of Kings and Lord of Lords. Therefore, I pledge allegiance to the throne of God. I will represent the constitution of God's government and live my life for the King and proclaim His Kingdom come, His will be done.

_____

_____
Date

Your Declaration of Dependence on God

Declaration #1

I am asking the Lord to teach me His ways and lead me in a plain path. As I wait on Him, I will be of good courage and allow Him to strengthen my heart in everything I do.

Psalm 27:11; Psalm 27:14

Declaration #2

This is the **last** year I will procrastinate. I will act upon every direction I receive from the Lord. I will complete every assignment without, slothfulness, hesitation, reservation or laziness. I will approach assignments and tasks with a spirit of excellence.

Deuteronomy 27:10; Jeremiah 26:13
2 Timothy 4:2; Colossians 4:17

Declaration #3

This is the **last** year my life will be stagnant. There will be progress in every area of my life.

Genesis 26:13
2 Peter 3:18

Declaration #4

I will make decisions based on God's directions. I will not be double-minded and where I lack wisdom, I will ask of God.

James 1:5, 8

Declaration #5

I will put on the whole armor of God so that I can stand against the wiles, tricks and deceptions of the devil. I will stand in truth, righteousness, peace, faith, salvation, prayer and on the Word of God.

Ephesians 6:4-16

Declaration #6

When trials, hardships and adversities come my way, I will be still and know in my heart that He is God. As I appreciate His mercy, kindness and love for me, I will commune in my heart and be still. As I stand, I will watch God bring victory in my life.

Psalm 4:4
Psalm 46:10

Declaration #7

This is the **last** year that I walk in fear or doubt because God has not given me the spirit of fear but of power and love and a sound mind. I will walk in holy boldness from this day forward.

II Timothy 1:7

Declaration #8

I will set my affections, my desires, my pursuits on the things above. I will seek God's Kingdom agenda first because I believe He will provide all the other things in my life.

Colossians 3:2
Matthew 6:33

Declaration #9

This is the **last year** I will have a weak prayer life. I will open my heart to prayer daily and seek the Lord through prayer for every area of my life.

Ephesians 6:18
Philippians 4:6

Declaration #10

This is the **last year** that I allow "stinking thinking" into my spirit. I will immediately shut down all negative language, gossip, backbiting, tattling, cursing, and anything like it before it has a chance to infiltrate my mind or spirit.

Galatians 5:19-21

Declaration #11

I will walk in the fruits of the spirit no matter the situation. I will walk in love, joy, peace, patience, kindness, goodness, faithfulness, gentleness, and self-control.

Galatians 5:22-23

Declaration #12

This is the **last year** I will allow the enemy to steal my joy through the adversities and trials of life. Happiness is fleeting, but joy is steadfast and it is from the Lord.

Nehemiah 8:10
Philippians 4:4

Declaration #13

I will "speak life" to every aspect of my life. I will speak those things that are not as though they are. Everything I ask for I will receive by faith.

Romans 4:17
James 1:6

Declaration #14

This year I am taking authority over my finances. I will be blessed in the city, and blessed in the country. The offspring of my body and everything I put my hands to will be blessed. I will be blessed coming in, and blessed when I go out. My goal is to become debt free so that I can be a blessing to the Kingdom of God.

Deuteronomy 28:3-6

Declaration #15

This year I will be more aware of my physical health. I will exercise more, eat well-balanced meals and get the rest my temple requires for health and be a living sacrifice that is acceptable to God.

1 Corinthians 6:19

Declaration #16

I will be more active in my place of worship. I will not be a pew hugger. I will take the **Matthew 11:12** mantle over my spiritual life. The Kingdom of Heaven suffers violence, but I will strive to take it back by spiritual force from the enemy. That means through prayer, fasting, right living, and being an example to others.

Declaration #17

I will trust in the Lord with my whole heart. I **will not** lean on my own understanding and in all things, I will acknowledge the Lord and allow Him to direct my paths.

Proverbs 3:5

Declaration #18

This year I will thank God for every situation in my life. I will bless Him when times are good and when times are bad. No matter the situation, I will bless the Lord at all times and His praise will continually be in my mouth.

Psalm 16:7; Psalm 26:12

Psalm 103:1-2; Psalm 115:18; Psalm 134:2

Declaration #19

I will approach my life from Psalm 139, "*Search me Oh Lord and know my heart, try me and know my thoughts and see if there be any wicked way in me.*" I will ask the Lord to show me the areas of my life that He desires to see change.

Psalm 139:23-24

Declaration #20

I will spend more time in prayer for my loved ones that do not know the Lord. I will ask the Lord to show me ways to share my relationship with Jesus so that they will want to know Him.

Matthew 5:16

Declaration #21

I will pursue the fullness of God in my life. I will not settle for less than His best in every aspect of my life. I will stand on every promise God has ever spoken to me.

Psalm 105:42

Declaration #22

This is the **last year** I will be a victim of "low level thinking." I will not live beneath my potential. I will seek the Lord for His best for me. I will believe God for great things.

Philippians 2:5

Declaration #23

This is the **last** year that I will live on the block called "pity." I have spent too many years feeling sorry for myself. I am more than a conqueror through Christ Jesus. Because of Christ Jesus, I have the victory!

Philippians 4:6

Declaration #24

I will take authority over my life. Jesus gave me authority to heal the sick, raise the dead and cast out demons. I will no longer hand my authority over to Satan. I will heal the sickness in my body, raise the dead places in my life and cast out all demonic activity in my life in the Name of Jesus.

Matthew 10:8

Declaration #25

I will press towards a "greater faith." The substance of my faith will begin with the Word of God. I will stand firm on the Word until the evidence happens.

Hebrews 11:1

Declaration #26

I will walk out my faith because faith, if it does not have works, deeds and actions of obedience to back it up, by itself is destitute of power inoperative, dead. I will walk by faith and not be sight.

2 Corinthians 5:7
James 2:17

Declaration #27

I will strive to please God through my faith because without faith it is impossible for me to please God. Anyone who comes to him must believe that he exists and that he rewards those who earnestly seek him; therefore, I will press to seek Him more.

Hebrews 11:6

Declaration #28

I will listen for the voice of the Lord in every area of my life. And I am asking Him to open the eyes of my heart so that I can see Him and everything around me with greater clarity.

Exodus 15:26; Psalms 29:3-4
1 Samuel 15:22; 2 Kings 6:17

Declaration #29

I am asking Christ to dwell in my heart through faith; and as I become rooted and grounded in love, I want to be able to comprehend what is the breadth and length and height and depth, and to know the love of Christ which surpasses knowledge, that I may be filled up to all the fullness of God.

Ephesians 3:17-19

Declaration #30

I believe God will do exceeding abundantly above all that I ask or think, according to the power that works in me.

Ephesians 3:20

Declaration #31

I will be a living testimony to the goodness of the Lord. I will be the salt and light the dark world needs to see. I will serve the Lord with gladness.

Matthew 5:13
Psalm 100

Declaration #32

This is the **last** year I will allow others to dictate my destiny. I will walk out the purpose and plan God has for me.

Jeremiah 29:11

Declaration #33

This is the **last** year that I will deal with the issues from my past. This is the year of completion for me. I will not drag dead weight into my new year, my new season or my new day.

Exodus 14:13

Declaration #34

I will be like a tree planted by the rivers of waters. I will bring forth fruit in my due season, my leaf will not wither and whatever I do will prosper.

Psalm 1
Psalms 92:13
Leviticus 28:9

Declaration #35

I **will not** participate in the "World Economic Recession," I am the head and not the tail. I have exceeding, abundantly, above all that I ask or think according to the power that works in me. I am recession proof through Christ Jesus.

Deuteronomy 28:13
Ephesians 3:20

Declaration #36

I will be a living sacrifice, holy and pleasing to God; this is my spiritual act of worship. I **will not** allow any one or anything to kill the light I carry within me.

Romans 12:1

Declaration #37

I will no longer be conformed to patterns of this world, but I will be transformed (changed) by the renewal of my mind [by its new ideals and its new attitude], so that I may prove what the will of God is, that which is good and acceptable and perfect.

Roman 12:2

Declaration #38

I will pursue my dreams. I will not allow the enemy to rob me of my destiny. I know that I can do all things through Christ who strengthens me.

Philippians 4:13

Declaration #39

I will give God the glory through my life. Apart from God, I am nothing and I can do nothing. With God, all things are possible in my life. To God be the Glory in all things.

John 15:5

Declaration #40

I will show more compassion for the poor, sick and needy. I will not judge a man simply because he is homeless. I will share with others the blessings of God. I am blessed to be a blessing.

Matthew 9:6
2 Corinthians 1:3
Acts 20:35

Declaration #41

I will spend at least 15 minutes a day in the Word of God. I will study to show myself approved to God, a workman who does not need to be ashamed and who correctly handles the word of truth.

2 Timothy 2:15

Declaration #42

I will be steadfast, immovable, and unshakeable in the work of the Lord, knowing that my labor is not in vain in the Lord. I will walk in compassion, but I will not compromise my faith, my integrity, or my relationship with the Lord.

1 Corinthians 15:58

Declaration #43

I will guard my mouth and I will think before I speak. I will avoid idle chatter. When angry, disturbed or annoyed, I will bridle my mouth. The words from my mouth will be words that glorify my Father in Heaven.

Psalm 39:1

Declaration #44

I will tell others about my church or ministry. I will share the good news of Jesus Christ. I will be the city on a hill.

Matthew 28:19
Mark 16:15

Declaration #45

I **will not** wonder or wander, instead I will start standing and commanding in the name of Jesus.

Mathew 10:1
Matthew 28:18
Luke 4:6

Declaration #46

I **will not** allow the voice of unbelief to infiltrate my spirit. I will not allow the spiritual penny pinchers to cause me to be a spiritual penny pincher. I will seek the fullness of God.

Matthew 13:58; Matthew 17:20
Mark 9:24; Romans 3:3

Declaration #47

Since worship is God's weapon of choice, I will use worship as my weapon of choice to confuse and defeat the enemy.

John 4:22-24

Declaration #48

I declare that the Lord is my Shepherd and I lack nothing in my life. The Lord makes me to lie down in green pastures. He renews my life and guides me in the right paths. I fear no harm because the Lord is with me. He is my comfort and my shield. Because He is my Shepherd, only goodness and mercy will pursue me all the days of my life.

Psalm 23

Declaration #49

I will set my hope on God and I will put my trust in Him. As you hear my cry, O God, Give heed to my prayer. From the end of the earth, I call to You when my heart is faint; lead me to the rock that is higher than I am. For You have been a refuge for me, a tower of strength against the enemy. Let me dwell in Your tent forever; let me take refuge in the shelter of Your wings for under your wings I find rest. My soul finds rest in God alone; my salvation comes from him. He alone is my rock and my salvation; He is my fortress, I will never be shaken.

Psalm 25: 1, 2, 15
Psalm 6:1-4
Psalm 62:1

Declaration #50

I will not allow the wounds from the past to remain open and hinder my destiny. I will seek the Lord for closure and pass any test that I have failed in the past. No longer will I allow spiritual bandages to cover my wounds. I will allow the Lord to open the wounds, heal, and deliver me. Once this is done, I pray that you will create in me a clean heart, O God, and renew a right, persevering, and steadfast spirit within me. Restore to me the joy of Your salvation and uphold me with a willing spirit. Then I will be a vessel ready for the Master's use.

John 8:36; Psalm 51:10
Psalm 51:12; 2 Timothy 2:21

Declaration #51

As I walk through this year, I will give no place to the devil in any area of my life. Whenever the enemy tries to come against me, I will take authority in Jesus Name and bind all demonic forces; for the weapons of my warfare are not physical [weapons of flesh and blood], but they are mighty before God for the overthrow and destruction of strongholds. I will demolish arguments and every pretension that sets itself up against the knowledge of God, and I will take captive every thought to make it obedient to Christ.

Ephesians 4:27
2 Corinthians 10:4 -5

Declaration #52

I declare that by signing this Declaration of Dependence on God, I know my God shall supply all my needs according to His riches in glory in Christ Jesus. I will seek first His kingdom and His righteousness, and all the things I desire will be given to me. When the enemy comes in like a flood The Spirit of the Lord will lift up a standard against him. I will cast my burdens on You LORD and You will sustain me because You will never allow the righteous to be shaken. I declare that I am an over comer by the Blood of the Lamb and by the word of my testimony.

Philippians 4:19; Matthew 6:33
Isaiah 59:19; Psalm 55:22
Revelation 12:11

Your Declaration of Dependence on God

The Word of God

For the word of God is quick, and powerful, and sharper than any two edged sword, piercing even to the dividing asunder of soul and spirit, and of the joints and marrow, and is a discerner of the thoughts and intents of the heart.

Hebrews 4:12

Chapter 8  Stand and See the Salvation of the Lord

Moses answered the people, "Do not be afraid. Stand firm and you will see the deliverance the LORD will bring you today. The Egyptians you see today you will never see again. The LORD will fight for you; you need only to be still" (Exodus 14:13-14).

Just as Moses told the children of Israel to fear not and stand firm, God is telling us today the same thing. Fear not and stand firm on the Word of God. While you are standing, you must guard your mind, heart and mouth.

The declaration of Moses to the people was based on faith and an unwavering trust in the God of our salvation. Moses declared that the Lord would fight for them, their only requirement was to be still. Moses made a declaration of deliverance that required looking past the overwhelming obstacles and seeing the Lord in the midst of the battle ready to deliver a great victory.

The Lord asked Moses, *"Why are you crying out to me? Tell the Israelites to move on."* Why are you wondering and wandering around trying to figure out your situation? Get on your face before God, listen for His direction, bridle your mouth and **move on!**

Your Declaration of Dependence on God

The greatest declaration the children of Israel could make was simply to move on. The greatest declaration you can make before the Lord is, "Lord, I trust you. I know you are with me. I will not walk in fear or doubt. I will stand and watch you bring victory to my life. I am more than a conqueror through Christ Jesus. Therefore, **I will move on**."

When you stand firm and allow the Lord to fight your battle you will be able to say, *the Egyptians [problems] I see today I will never see again.*

As you begin to renew your mind to speak the Word of God over your life, remember that you need not be afraid because He is Jehovah Shammah, the Lord is There. Stand firm and you will see the deliverance the LORD will bring you. The LORD will fight for you; you need only to be still and trust the Lord to bring you victory.

"And the name of the city from that time on will be: THE LORD IS THERE.
Ezekiel 48:35

As you move to your next level in the Lord commit to trusting Him with all your heart, cease to lean on your own understanding and in all your ways acknowledging Him, the Lord will make your paths straight (Proverbs 3:5-6 *Paraphrased*). You will be able stand firm in faith and trust and *"You will also decree a thing, and it will be established for you; and light will shine on your ways* (Job 22:28).

Your Declaration of Dependence on God

If you declare failure - failure will follow, but if you stand and declare victory through Christ Jesus, God will establish victory for you. And the light, the glory of God will shine on your ways, your path and your destiny. *But thanks be to God, Who gives us the victory [making us conquerors] through our Lord Jesus Christ (1Corinthians 15:57 AMP).*

Guard your mouth and MOVE ON! Do not look back at the situation, move forward and possess the destiny that the Lord has spoken into your life before the foundation of the world. TRUST GOD AND MOVE ON!!

> *As you enter the final chapter of this workbook, it is important to begin breaking the word curses you have spoken in the past. This is vital to renewing your mind to the newness of your relationship with Christ Jesus. You must renounce every curse that you have spoken over yourself, children, spouse, finances, etc.*
>
> *Read Psalm 51 and pray the Psalms 139 prayer before you begin the Prayer for Breaking Word Curses. They can be found in the back of this book in the Scriptures on Prayer section.*

Your Declaration of Dependence on God

Your Declaration of Dependence on God

Chapter 9

A Prayer for Breaking Curses

Heavenly Father, I come to you in the name of Jesus. I repent of any words that I have spoken that have cursed any person, place or thing.

I ask you to forgive me for speaking a curse over any person, place or thing. I renounce (call out word curse) and every word curse that I have spoken over (name person or persons) and break the spine of all the curses and revoke and nullify them. I release (name person or persons) from any hindrances that my words have caused.

I bless you to prosper (name person or persons). I bless you to be all God intended for you to be. I bless you to be an encouragement for others. I bless you to be able to bless others.

Your Declaration of Dependence on God

People - I bless you to love as Jesus loves. I bless you to forgive as Jesus does. I bless you to grow in your spirit to draw closer to God.

Places - I bless you to be a place of joy. I bless you to have God's people around. I bless you to be a restful place for people, and a safe place. I bless you to be a place of beauty.

Things - I bless you to prosperity, to function as you were intended. I bless you to operate in a safe and true manner. I bless you to be valuable and useful. I bless you to be an asset not a deficit. I bless you to increase in worth.[1]

Your Declaration of Dependence on God

Chapter 10

DECLARATION JOURNAL

#_____

Your Declaration of Dependence on God

DECLARATION JOURNAL #_____

Your Declaration of Dependence on God

DECLARATION JOURNAL #_____

Your Declaration of Dependence on God

DECLARATION JOURNAL #_____

Your Declaration of Dependence on God

DECLARATION JOURNAL #_____

Your Declaration of Dependence on God

DECLARATION JOURNAL #_____

Your Declaration of Dependence on God

DECLARATION JOURNAL #_____

Your Declaration of Dependence on God

DECLARATION JOURNAL #_____

Your Declaration of Dependence on God

DECLARATION JOURNAL #_____

Your Declaration of Dependence on God

DECLARATION JOURNAL #_____

Your Declaration of Dependence on God

DECLARATION JOURNAL #_____

Your Declaration of Dependence on God

DECLARATION JOURNAL #_____

Your Declaration of Dependence on God

DECLARATION JOURNAL #_____

Your Declaration of Dependence on God

DECLARATION JOURNAL #_____

Your Declaration of Dependence on God

DECLARATION JOURNAL #_____

Your Declaration of Dependence on God

DECLARATION JOURNAL #_____

Your Declaration of Dependence on God

DECLARATION JOURNAL #_____

Your Declaration of Dependence on God

DECLARATION JOURNAL #_____

Your Declaration of Dependence on God

DECLARATION JOURNAL #_____

Your Declaration of Dependence on God

DECLARATION JOURNAL #_____

Your Declaration of Dependence on God

DECLARATION JOURNAL #_____

Your Declaration of Dependence on God

DECLARATION JOURNAL #_____

Your Declaration of Dependence on God

DECLARATION JOURNAL #_____

Your Declaration of Dependence on God

DECLARATION JOURNAL #_____

Your Declaration of Dependence on God

DECLARATION JOURNAL #_____

Your Declaration of Dependence on God

DECLARATION JOURNAL #_____

Your Declaration of Dependence on God

DECLARATION JOURNAL #_____

Your Declaration of Dependence on God

DECLARATION JOURNAL #_____

Your Declaration of Dependence on God

DECLARATION JOURNAL #_____

Your Declaration of Dependence on God

DECLARATION JOURNAL #_____

Your Declaration of Dependence on God

DECLARATION JOURNAL #_____

Your Declaration of Dependence on God

DECLARATION JOURNAL #_____

Your Declaration of Dependence on God

DECLARATION JOURNAL #_____

Your Declaration of Dependence on God

DECLARATION JOURNAL #_____

Your Declaration of Dependence on God

DECLARATION JOURNAL #_____

Your Declaration of Dependence on God

DECLARATION JOURNAL #_____

Your Declaration of Dependence on God

DECLARATION JOURNAL #_____

Your Declaration of Dependence on God

DECLARATION JOURNAL #_____

Your Declaration of Dependence on God

DECLARATION JOURNAL #_____

Your Declaration of Dependence on God

DECLARATION JOURNAL #_____

Your Declaration of Dependence on God

DECLARATION JOURNAL #_____

Your Declaration of Dependence on God

DECLARATION JOURNAL #_____

Your Declaration of Dependence on God

DECLARATION JOURNAL #_____

Your Declaration of Dependence on God

DECLARATION JOURNAL #_____

Your Declaration of Dependence on God

DECLARATION JOURNAL #_____

Your Declaration of Dependence on God

DECLARATION JOURNAL #_____

Your Declaration of Dependence on God

DECLARATION JOURNAL #_____

Your Declaration of Dependence on God

DECLARATION JOURNAL #_____

Your Declaration of Dependence on God

DECLARATION JOURNAL #_____

Your Declaration of Dependence on God

DECLARATION JOURNAL #_____

Your Declaration of Dependence on God

DECLARATION JOURNAL #_____

Your Declaration of Dependence on God

DECLARATION JOURNAL #_____

Your Declaration of Dependence on God

Chapter 11

Prayer Scriptures

Then the Levitical priests arose and blessed the people; and their voice was heard and their **prayer** came to His holy dwelling place, to heaven.

2 Chronicles 30:27

Let Your ear now be attentive and Your eyes open to hear the **prayer** of Your servant which I am praying before You now, day and night, on behalf of the sons of Israel Your servants, confessing the sins of the sons of Israel which we have sinned against You; I and my father's house have sinned.

Nehemiah 1:6

Answer me when I call, O God of my righteousness! You have relieved me in my distress; Be gracious to me and hear my **prayer**.

Psalm 4:1

Heed the sound of my cry for help, my King and my God, For to You I **pray**. In the morning, O LORD, You will hear my voice; In the morning, I will order *my prayer* to You and *eagerly* watch.

Psalm 5:2-3

Therefore, let everyone who is godly pray to You in a time when You may be found; Surely, in a flood of great waters they will not reach him. You are my hiding place; You preserve me from trouble; You surround me with songs of deliverance. Selah

Psalm 32:6-7

The LORD will command His loving kindness in the daytime; And His song will be with me in the night, A **prayer** to the God of my life.

Psalm 42:8

Hear my cry, O God; Give heed to my **prayer**. From the end of the earth I call to You when my heart is faint; Lead me to the rock that is higher than I For You have been a refuge for me, A tower of strength against the enemy. Let me dwell in Your tent forever; Let me take refuge in the shelter of Your wings. Selah.

Psalm 61:1-4

Your Declaration of Dependence on God

"When you **pray**, you are not to be like the hypocrites; for they love to stand and **pray** in the synagogues and on the street corners so that they may be seen by men. Truly, I say to you, they have their reward in full. "But you, when you **pray,** go into your inner room, close your door and **pray** to your Father who is in secret, and your Father who sees *what is done* in secret will reward you. "And when you are praying, do not use meaningless repetition as the Gentiles do, for they suppose that they will be heard for their many words. "So do not be like them; for your Father knows what you need before you ask Him. " **Pray**, then, in this way: 'Our Father who is in heaven, Hallowed be Your name. ' Your kingdom come. Your will be done, On earth as it is in heaven. ' Give us this day our daily bread. 'And forgive us our debts, as we also have forgiven our debtors. 'And do not lead us into temptation, but deliver us from evil. [For Yours is the kingdom and the power and the glory forever. Amen.]' " For if you forgive others for their transgressions, your heavenly Father will also forgive you. "But if you do not forgive others, then your Father will not forgive your transgressions.

Matt. 6:5-15

" But this kind does not go out except by **prayer** and fasting."

Matt. 17:21

It was at this time that He went off to the mountain to pray, and He spent the whole night in **prayer** to God.

Luke 6:12

When He rose from **prayer**, He came to the disciples and found them sleeping from sorrow, and said to them, "Why are you sleeping? Get up and pray that you may not enter into temptation."

Luke 22:45-46

With all **prayer and petition pray at all times in the Spirit, and with this in view, be on the alert with** all perseverance and petition for all the saints, and *pray* on my behalf, that utterance may be given to me in the opening of my mouth, to make known with boldness the mystery of the gospel,

Eph. 6:18-19

Be anxious for nothing, but in everything by **prayer** and supplication with thanksgiving let your requests be made known to God. And the peace of God, which surpasses all comprehension, will guard your hearts and your minds in Christ Jesus.

Phil. 4:6-7

Devote yourselves to **prayer**, keeping alert in it with *an attitude of* thanksgiving.

Colossians 4:2

Your Declaration of Dependence on God

For everything created by God is good, and nothing is to be rejected if it is received with gratitude; for it is sanctified by means of the word of God and **prayer**.
1 Timothy 4:4-5

Is anyone among you suffering? *Then* he must pray. Is anyone cheerful? He is to sing praises. Is anyone among you sick? *Then* he must call for the elders of the church and they are to pray over him, anointing him with oil in the name of the Lord; and the **prayer** offered in faith will restore the one who is sick, and the Lord will raise him up, and if he has committed sins, they will be forgiven him.
Therefore, confess your sins to one another, and pray for one another so that you may be healed. The effective **prayer** of a righteous man can accomplish much.
James 5:13-16

I thank my God always, making mention of you in my **prayers**, because I hear of your love and of the faith which you have toward the Lord Jesus and toward all the saints; *and I pray* that the fellowship of your faith may become effective through the knowledge of every good thing which is in you for Christ's sake.
Philemon 1:4-4-6

You husbands in the same way, live with *your wives* in an understanding way, as with someone weaker, since she is a woman; and show her honor as a fellow heir of the grace of life, so that your **prayers** will not be hindered.
1 Peter 3:7

"FOR THE EYES OF THE LORD ARE TOWARD THE RIGHTEOUS, AND HIS EARS ATTEND TO THEIR **PRAYER**, BUT THE FACE OF THE LORD IS AGAINST THOSE WHO DO EVIL."
1 Peter 3:12

Your Declaration of Dependence on God

Your Declaration of Dependence on God

Declarative Prayers

Shattering Strongholds Prayer

Psalm 139 Prayer

Prayer of Deliverance

Prayer of Salvation

Your Declaration of Dependence on God

Shattering Strongholds Prayer

Heavenly Father, In the Name and authority of Jesus Christ and by the power of His shed Blood, you are my battle-axe and my weapon of war. With you, O Lord, I shatter infirmities, sickness, disease and death.

With you, I shatter fear, rejection, pride, unbelief, doubt, bitterness, torment, anger, confusion and unforgiveness, jealous and envy.

With you, I shatter poverty, lack, debt and financial destruction.

With you, I shatter spiritual and physical abortions and miscarriages.

With you, I shatter abuse, lust, rape, and incest.

With you, I shatter spousal abuse, adultery, fornication, divorce and separation.

With you, I shatter compromise, laziness and slothfulness.

With you, I shatter addictions, perversions, obsessions, cravings and lust.

With you, I shatter chains, cords, shackles, spells, and curses over my life and my family.

With you, I shatter counterfeit shepherds and itching eared flocks.

With you, I shatter false prophets, false teachers, false anointing and temple harlots.

Your Declaration of Dependence on God

With you, I shatter the Spirit of Competition, Spirit of Jezebel, Spirit of Absalom, Spirit of Ananias & Sapphira, Spirit of Leviathan, Spirit of Belial, Spirit of Carnality, Spirit of Fear, Spirit of Compromise, Spirit of Jealousy, Spirit of Pride, and Spirit of Anti-Christ that are infiltrating the church.

With you, I shatter false anointing and release Your anointing to destroy the yokes of bondage.

With you, I shatter all chains, cords, shackles, spells, and curses over my church.

With you, I shatter corrupt city, state and federal governments and governmental officials.

With you, I shatter all chains, cords, shackles, spells, and curses over our city, state and federal government.

Through the Blood of Jesus, I loose myself, my family, my church, my city, my state and all governmental agencies from the bondages of the enemy and command the spirits that once controlled these areas back to the pits of hell, never to return. In the name of Jesus.

According to Galatians 3:13, I have been redeemed from *"the curse of the law"* by the sacrifice of Jesus. I exercise my faith in the power of the shed Blood of Jesus, destroy every stronghold of the enemy, and loose myself from every curse.

Your Declaration of Dependence on God

Lord, I thank you for setting me free from every curse and every spirit that has operated in my life, church, and government. I thank you that we are free to love, obey and worship you.

We will be still, and know that You are God; You will be exalted among the nations, You will be exalted in the earth" (Psalm 46:10). In the Name of Jesus. Amen.

Your Declaration of Dependence on God

Psalm 139 Prayer

O Lord, You are my God, You know when I sit down and when I rise up; You understand my thoughts. You are intimately acquainted with all my ways. Even before there is a word on my tongue, Behold, O LORD, You know it all. Where can I go from Your Spirit? Where can I flee from Your presence? If I ascend to heaven, You are there; If I make my bed in Hell, You are there. If I take the wings of the dawn, If I dwell in the farthest part of the sea, Even there Your hand will lead me, And Your right hand will lay hold of me. As I begin this journey of discovering the issues in my life that keep me from your fullness I ask you in the Name of Jesus to Search me, O God, and know my heart; Try me and know my thoughts; And see if there be any hurtful way in me, And lead me in the everlasting way.

Your Declaration of Dependence on God

Prayer of Deliverance

Heavenly Father, I repent of any sins in my life or my ancestors' lives that have resulted in a curse. I repent of all disobedience, rebellion, perversion, witchcraft, idolatry, lust, adultery, fornication, mistreatment of others, murder, cheating, lying, sorcery, divination, and occult involvement. I ask for Your forgiveness and cleansing through the blood of the Lord Jesus Christ.

I take authority over and break any and every curse upon my life in the Name of Jesus. I break all curses of poverty, lack, debt, destruction, sickness, death, and vagabondism. I break all curses on my marriage, family, children, and relationships. I break curses of rejection, pride, rebellion, lust hurt, incest, rape, Ahab, Jezebel, fear, insanity, madness, and confusion.

I break all curses affecting my finances, mind, sexual character, emotions, will, and relationships.

I break every jinx, hex, spell and spoken curse over my life.

I break every fetter, shackle, chain, cord, habit, and cycle that is the result of a curse.

Your Declaration of Dependence on God

According to Galatians 3:13, I have been redeemed from *"the curse of the law"* by the sacrifice of Jesus. I exercise my faith in the blood of Jesus and loose my descendants and myself from any and every curse. I claim forgiveness through the blood of Jesus for the sins of the fathers.

All my sins have been remitted, and I loose myself from the curses that came because of disobedience and rebellion to the Word of God.

I exercise my faith, and I know that confession is made unto salvation (Romans 10:10). Therefore, I confess that Abraham's blessings are mine (Galatians 3:14). I am not cursed, but blessed. I am *"the head, and not the tail"* (Deuteronomy 28:13). I am blessed coming in and blessed going out. I am blessed, and what God has blessed cannot be cursed.

I command spirits of rejection, hurt, bitterness, unforgiveness, bondage, torment, death, destruction, fear, lust, perversion, mind control, witchcraft, poverty, lack, debt, confusion, double-mindlessness, sickness, infirmity, pain, divorce, separation, loneliness, self-pity, self-destruction, self-rejection, anger, rage, wrath, anguish, vagabondism, abuse, and addiction to come out in the name of Jesus!

Lord, I thank you for setting me free from every curse and every spirit that has operated in my life as a result of a curse. Amen.[21]

Your Declaration of Dependence on God

Prayer of Salvation

No matter what you do in life, nothing else will matter except your relationship with Jesus Christ. A committed relationship with Jesus is the key to a victorious life. Our Lord and Savior Jesus Christ laid down His life for us. He rose again for us so that we could spend eternity with Him. Jesus said, *"I am come that they might have life, and that they might have it more abundantly."*

It is God's will that everyone receive eternal salvation. The only way to receive salvation is to call upon the name of Jesus, confess Him as Lord of your life. The Bible says in Romans 10:9-13, that if thou shalt confess with thy mouth the Lord Jesus, and shalt believe in thine heart that God hath raised him from the dead, thou shalt be saved. *For with the heart man believeth unto righteousness; and with the mouth, confession is made unto salvation. For the scripture saith, whosoever believeth on him shall not be ashamed. For there is no difference between the Jew and the Greek: for the same Lord over all is rich unto all that call upon him. For whosoever shall call upon the name of the Lord shall be saved.*

God loves you--no matter who you are, no matter what your past. God loves you so much that He gave His one and only begotten Son for you. The Bible tells us *"...whoever believes in him shall not perish but have eternal life"* (John 3:16 NIV). Jesus laid down His life and rose again so that we could spend eternity with Him in heaven and experience His absolute best on earth. If you would like to receive Jesus into your life, say the following

Your Declaration of Dependence on God

prayer aloud. It is vital that you mean it from your heart.

Heavenly Father, I come to You admitting that I am a sinner. Right now, I choose to turn away from sin, and I ask You to cleanse me of all unrighteousness. I believe that Your Son, Jesus, died on the cross to take away my sins. I also believe that He rose again from the dead so that I may be justified and made righteous through faith in Him. I call upon the name of Jesus Christ to be the Savior of my life. Jesus, I choose to follow You, and I ask that You fill me with the power of the Holy Spirit. I declare right now that I am a born-again child of God. I am free from sin, and full of the righteousness of God. I am saved in Jesus' name. Amen.

If you prayed this prayer to receive Jesus Christ as your Lord and Savior or if this book has blessed your life, we would like to hear from you. Please write us: Igniting the Fire Publishing
1314 North 38th Street, Suite 101
Kansas City, KS 66102
Or
It Is Written Ministries
1314 North 38th Street, Suite 102
Kansas City, KS 66102

Your Declaration of Dependence on God

Appendix
Sample of Self-Life Issues

Self-absorbed	preoccupied with self: excessively concerned with your own life and interests
Self-abuse	masturbation when viewed as being detrimental to character
Self-annihilation	suicide: an act or instance of suicide
Self-assured	behaving in a relaxed manner that displays confidence that your views\abilities are of value
Self-centered	thinking only of self: tending to concentrate selfishly on your own needs and affairs
Self-conceit	swelled head, pride, self-satisfaction, vanity, arrogance, self-importance
Self-convicting	finding guilt in yourself, condemning yourself
Self-deception	delusion, fantasy, self-delusion, self-deception,
Self-defeating	thwarting own objectives: defeating the very objective or purpose it is designed to serve
Self-righteous	sanctimonious, smug, pious, haughty, hoity-toity (disapproving), hypocritical, pretentious, holier-than-thou (informal), pompous
Self-seeking	selfish: interested only in gaining an advantage over others, not in sharing or cooperating
Self-serving	lacking consideration of others: putting personal concerns & interests before others
Self-will	stubbornness: stubborn determination to hold to personal views and behavior
Self-vindication	Overly defensive of yourself
Selfish	concerned with your own interests, needs, and wishes while ignoring those of others

This is a sample list. For a complete list of self-life issues, pick up a copy of my audio book
The Enemy in Me: Overcoming Self Life-Issues.

About the Author

God has called Jacquie Hadnot to encourage, inspire, motivate and activate the gifts of the Spirit in order to raise powerful ministries in the body of Christ. She is becoming a voice on the subject of prayer, worship and spiritual warfare.

She is recognized as a modern-day apostle with a strong prophetic and psalmist anointing. She has a revelational teaching ministry with a mandate to saturate the world with the Word of God. Jacquie's heart is to see people arise and walk in the destiny and inheritance of the Lord.

She has founded and established It Is Written Ministries, a publication company, an accounting and consulting firm, and a global radio station. As a retired accountant and financial executive, Jacquie blends ministerial and entrepreneurial applications in her ministry to enrich and empower a diverse audience with skills and abilities to take kingdoms for the Lord Jesus Christ. A lecturer, conference speaker, teacher, business trainer, and financial consultant, she provides consulting services to businesses, churches, and individuals. She has written over twenty-five books, manuals, and other materials on intimacy with God, prayer, fasting and spiritual warfare. She has also released several music Cds and received numerous music and book publishing awards.

Your Declaration of Dependence on God

Beyond the pulpit, Jacquie is a talk-show host on both television and radio with her own program, Light for Your Path. Weekly she applies God's wisdom to today's world solutions. Her ministry goal is to make Christ's teachings relevant for today. She also publishes a quarterly magazine by the same name.

In addition to her vast experience, Jacquie has a Th.d. in Pastoral Theology and an M.min. in Ministry Leadership. She is also a wife, mother of one daughter and grandmother of one grandson. She and her husband, Gregory presently pastor It Is Written Ministries in Kansas City Kansas. They also serve as owners and corporate officers of Igniting the Fire Media Group.

Your Declaration of Dependence on God

Other Books & Materials by Dr. Jacquie

Books in Print

The Art of Spiritual Warfare: Strategies for Effective Spiritual Warfare

The Extravagant Love of God: Experiencing the Prophetic Flow of God

Cry Aloud, Spare Not! A Prophetic Call to the Fast God Has Chosen for You

Cry Aloud, Spare Not! The Companion-Study Guide

His Mercy Endures Forever: Psalms, Prayers & Meditations for the Heart

To Make War with the Saints; Satan's Kingdom Agenda

A Treasure in the Pleasure of Loving God

Loving God through His Names: 365 Days of the Year

Closing the Doors to Satan's Attacks: *Overcoming Fear*

Where Is Your God? Have We Lost the Referential Fear of the Lord?

Audio Books & Teachings

Are You in Position? Alignment + Assignment = Advancement

The Harlot Heart

Dimensional Faith

Don't Blame Satan: God is Up to Something

One Thing…

Pursing His Presence in the Midst of Pain

When Your Faith Is Being Tested

Trusting God in Your Season of Discouragement

More of You: The Prophetic Flow of Prayer (Volume 1)

In the Face of Adversity: *Overcoming Life's Storms*

Be Not Deceived…

Where Is Your God?

Recognizing Your Due Season

Praying the Healing Scriptures

The Enemy in Me: *Overcoming Self-Life Issues*

Your Declaration of Dependence on God

Music CD

The Extravagant Love of God

His Mercy Endures Forever: Praying the Psalms

The Spoken Word of Love

Igniting the Fire Compilation CD

DVD Series

When Your Faith is Being Tested

What Made David Run

Pregnant With A Purpose: Birthing Your Dreams Volume 1

Agents of Change

Virtuous Women of Worship

Booklets

- When Fear Crept In
- Deeper…
- Naked, Broken and Unashamed

Visit my website for a complete list of teachings.

Live in His Presence, breathe in His Presence, love in His Presence, stay thirsty for His presence.

Your Declaration of Dependence on God

End each day with Prayer.

...and My people who are called by My name humble themselves and pray and seek My face and turn from their wicked ways, then I will hear from heaven, will forgive their sin and will heal their land. "Now My eyes will be open and My ears attentive to the prayer offered in this place.

(2 Chronicles 7:14-15)

Your Declaration of Dependence on God

Declaration of Dependence on God

Share with Family and Friends

~~~~~~~~~~~~~~~~~~~~~~~~~~~~~~~~~~~~~

Heavenly Father, In the Name and authority of Jesus Christ and by the power of His shed Blood,

I agree that from this day forward I will begin to speak life into every situation I encounter. Job 22:28 declares that I shall decree a thing, and it shall be established for me: and the light of the Lord will shall shine on my ways.

In the Name and authority of Jesus Christ and by the power of His shed Blood, I will decree the power of God and the favor of God over my life and it will be established for me by Christ Jesus.

I declare that I represent the King of Kings and Lord of Lords. Therefore, I pledge allegiance to the throne of God. I will represent the constitution of God's government and live my life for the King and proclaim His Kingdom come, His will be done.

_____

                                     _____

                                            Date

Your Declaration of Dependence on God

Declaration of Dependence on God

Share with Family and Friends

~~~~~~~~~~~~~~~~~~~~~~~~~~~~~~~~~~~~

Heavenly Father, In the Name and authority of Jesus Christ and by the power of His shed Blood,

I agree that from this day forward I will begin to speak life into every situation I encounter. Job 22:28 declares that I shall decree a thing, and it shall be established for me: and the light of the Lord will shall shine on my ways.

In the Name and authority of Jesus Christ and by the power of His shed Blood, I will decree the power of God and the favor of God over my life and it will be established for me by Christ Jesus.

I declare that I represent the King of Kings and Lord of Lords. Therefore, I pledge allegiance to the throne of God. I will represent the constitution of God's government and live my life for the King and proclaim His Kingdom come, His will be done.

_____

_____
Date

Your Declaration of Dependence on God

Declaration of Dependence on God

Share with Family and Friends

~~~~~~~~~~~~~~~~~~~~~~~~~~~~~~~~~~~~~~~

Heavenly Father, In the Name and authority of Jesus Christ and by the power of His shed Blood,

I agree that from this day forward I will begin to speak life into every situation I encounter. Job 22:28 declares that I shall decree a thing, and it shall be established for me: and the light of the Lord will shall shine on my ways.

In the Name and authority of Jesus Christ and by the power of His shed Blood, I will decree the power of God and the favor of God over my life and it will be established for me by Christ Jesus.

I declare that I represent the King of Kings and Lord of Lords. Therefore, I pledge allegiance to the throne of God. I will represent the constitution of God's government and live my life for the King and proclaim His Kingdom come, His will be done.

_____

_____
Date

Your Declaration of Dependence on God

Declaration of Dependence on God

Share with Family and Friends

~~~~~~~~~~~~~~~~~~~~~~~~~~~~~~~~~~~~

Heavenly Father, In the Name and authority of Jesus Christ and by the power of His shed Blood,

I agree that from this day forward I will begin to speak life into every situation I encounter. Job 22:28 declares that I shall decree a thing, and it shall be established for me: and the light of the Lord will shall shine on my ways.

In the Name and authority of Jesus Christ and by the power of His shed Blood, I will decree the power of God and the favor of God over my life and it will be established for me by Christ Jesus.

I declare that I represent the King of Kings and Lord of Lords. Therefore, I pledge allegiance to the throne of God. I will represent the constitution of God's government and live my life for the King and proclaim His Kingdom come, His will be done.

_____

_____

Date

Your Declaration of Dependence on God

[1] Prayers. Page 205, Edition 7.

Your Declaration of Dependence on God

www.ingramcontent.com/pod-product-compliance
Lightning Source LLC
LaVergne TN
LVHW061342060426
835512LV00016B/2628